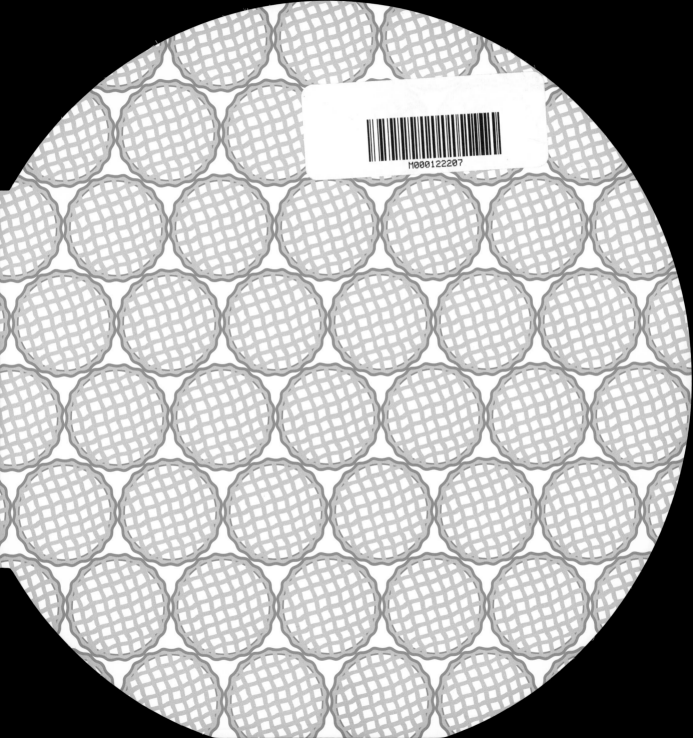

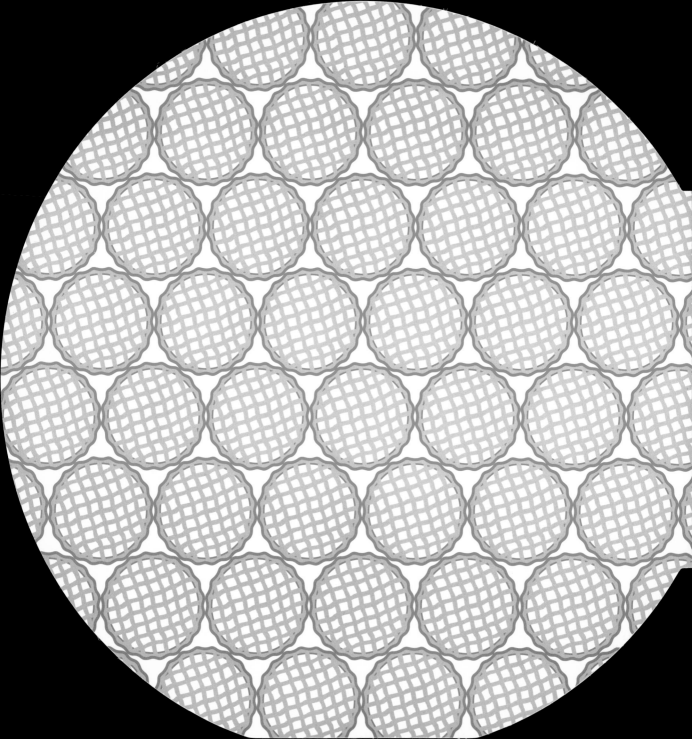

TARTS AND PIES

50 Easy Recipes

ACADEMIA
BARILLA

EDITED BY

ACADEMIA BARILLA

PHOTOGRAPHY BY

ALBERTO ROSSI
CHEF MARIO GRAZIA
CHEF MARIO STROLLO
CHEF LUCA ZANGA

RECIPES BY

CHEF MARIO GRAZIA

TEXT BY

MARIAGRAZIA VILLA

GRAPHIC DESIGN

MARINELLA DEBERNARDI

EDITORIAL COORDINATION ACADEMIA BARILLA

CHATO MORANDI
ILARIA ROSSI
LEANNE KOSINSKI

CONTENTS

5

THE CRUMBLY PLEASURE
OF A PIE

*Good apple pies are a considerable
part of our domestic happiness.*

Jane Austen, British writer

It's grandmother's cake *par excellence*. The good, simple sweet from the time when we were children and its aroma from the oven brought us all the kitchen. We enjoyed it at breakfast, for afternoon tea, after lunch and finally after dinner. In short, at every moment when we needed a real cuddle. The golden, crumbly shortcrust pastry, which held a soft filling and mingled on the surface with the classical diamond motif, made us feel protected and safe, at home. And the filling? In some way sweet, it reminded us that we were little and had the right to a sweet, pleasant gesture.

To remember a tart, in its numerous variations, is to remember someone who in our childhood thought of us. It is the aroma of family and affection that Grandma Duck communicated with her mythical apple pie. The one that she left to cool on the windowsill of the farmhouse, the one whose aroma spread for miles and miles... attracting the grandchildren Huey, Dewey and Louie, but more often the hungry great nephew Gus the Goose and Humphrey the Bear. But it is also the sense of childhood and gaiety of the tarts that appear, with tea and cakes, on the well-laid table of the Mad Hatter and the White Rabbit for Alice in Wonderland, to celebrate his Non-Birthday... Festive and carefree, they evoke unexpected surprises.

In the Beginning, there Was a Legend
It seems that the history of the tart is rooted in the Pre-Christian era and is the fruit of a heartwarming episode: overpowering love and the pain of being unrequited, the sensitivity of giving one's talents to those who can appreciate

them and the deep gratitude of those who receive them, the creativity of those who transmute gratitude into something sweet and the generosity of those who wish to share it with others.

In fact, a legend recounts that the beautiful mermaid Parthenope fell in love with Ulysses and that he rejected her. Driven by pain, the gentle marine creature killed herself in the Gulf of Naples, to be precise where Castel dell'Ovo stands. Every year, however, in spring she was reborn from the waters to entertain the people of the place with her melodious song.

In order to thank her for that sweet gift, which was renewed every year with the advent of spring, the people of the Gulf decided to offer her flour, the symbol and riches of the country, ricotta, the present of pastors and the present of shepherds and sheep, eggs, the metaphor of the rebirth of life, of grain boiled in milk, the sign of the union between the vegetable and animal kingdoms, a little orange blossom water, the homage of the earth, candied citrus fruits and spices to represent distant peoples, and sugar, so similar to her voice. The mermaid took these gifts and dived deep to take them to the feet of the gods, who combined them and, *voilà*, created the first tart in history: the Neapolitan Pastiera.

Then Parthenope, rather than tasting it, rose from the depths and donated the tart, whose sweetness exceeded even her song, to the generous inhabitants of the Gulf, as a sign of gratitude.

What Really Happened?

The Pastiera, the symbol of Neapolitan pastry making, was the first historically documented tart similar to modern tarts, in the sense of embrace between shortcrust pastry and filling. Certainly, this kind of cake already existed in the popular tradition, moreover with the mystical meaning of symbol of the

resurrection of Christ (still today in Naples, this tart is prepared on Good Friday), created by the Nuns of the Convent of San Gregorio Armeno during the Middle Ages.

From the end of the nineteenth century, however, we learn the documented episode of Ferdinand II of the Two Sicilies, who had his wife Maria Theresa of Hapsburg-Teschen, so merry as to be called "the queen who never smiles," try a slice of this delicious Easter cake: she, taken with the specialty... at last smiled!

A Still More Ancient Story ...

The tart is one of the historic elements of Italian pastry-making, together with the fried delicacies, cookies and wafers, raised *pandolci*, with non-leavened cakes based on nuts and candied fruits and the wide range of creams and ice creams.

A descendant of the concept, as would term it today, of two rural foods typical of Ancient Rome, the "obleidos," the wafers that were quickly cooked when necessary and spread with honey, flour *focacce* bread, a sort of shell on which people placed pieces of cooked fruit, like apples, pears, pomegranates, grapes, figs or plums (just as today we spread jam or creams), the tart spread in nobles' banquets and monasteries from the High Middle Ages onwards, when it often presented a cream cheese filling (thus a savory ingredient), honey, spices and candied fruits (precursor of what would be the Sicilian Cassata).

However, it would only be in the following centuries that the tart would acquire a sweeter meaning, also incorporating those new ingredients which came from the Orient or the Americas, like sugar (brown sugar, imported from the Arab lands as a spice from 900 C.E., then replaced by beet sugar at the end of the eighteenth century), the divine cocoa, coffee, cinnamon or vanilla.

The Sweetness of Home

The tart is certainly the most famous homemade Italian cake. It is quick and easy to prepare and to cook, everyone likes it, it is versatile, because it can be filled in a thousand different ways and the pastry can always be enriched by new ingredients, and it is suitable for every situation, from the most everyday ones to special occasions, like parties, birthdays and family anniversaries.

A few genuine ingredients to make the shortcrust pastry (in some recipes the pastry may be short pastry or puff pastry), sometimes flavored with cocoa, almonds, hazelnuts, coconut or other flavors, which will welcome a potentially infinite range of fillings: jam, custard, lemon, chocolate, coffee, chestnut or ricotta, fresh or dried fruit ...

It can be whole or subdivided into many little tarts, which are ideal to offer to guests during a formal event, can be baked in round or rectangular molds, can be open or closed by a disk of pastry, and thus contain a filling, can be covered by a meringue or by a crumble of nut shortcrust pastry, or can be turned upside-down when, in preparing it one starts from placing the filling and then the pastry in the baking pan and turns it upside-down after baking.

Italian Tarts, and Not Only Italian

Academia Barilla, the international centre dedicated to spreading Italian cuisine, has selected fifty tart recipes for this book. From the classical ones, with fresh fruit and jam, to the most tempting, the real passion of old and young, made with chocolate, custard and nuts, to the delicious shortcrust tarts with fillings, either meringue or upside-down.

The book ranges from extremely simple preparations to more elaborate ones, from traditional recipes to more creative ones which combine, for instance, fruit and herbs, like Peach and Rosemary Tart, use vegetables, like the Pumpkin

and Hazelnut Tart, or give value to an ingredient which is traditionally not common in pastry-making, like extra virgin olive oil, perhaps combining it with gianduja chocolate.

They are not only delicacies of Italian ancestry, like the tart of apples, rice and pine nuts called "Grandma's," but also recipes created elsewhere which, however, share with Italian pastries the high quality of raw materials, felicitous combinations and convivial spirit. The upside-down apple cake, or Tarte Tatin, is a typical French upside-down tart, in which the apples are caramelized in butter and sugar before cooking. It seems to have been created at the end of the nineteenth century by the sisters Stephanie and Caroline Tatin, who ran a hotel-restaurant for hunters at Lamotte-Beuvron in the heart of France: one of the two sisters forgot to place the short pastry under the apples, and after they were caramelized, thought of remedying the mistake by putting the pastry on top of the mixture obtained, then of putting the tart back in the oven and upturning it on a serving dish.

The Crostata Linzer (Linz Tart), on the other hand, also called "Linzertorte" (Linz Cake), is a traditional Austrian delicacy, which originated in the city of Linz, where it is usually prepared over Christmas. It has almond or hazelnut shortcrust pastry, flavored with vanilla or cinnamon and filled with currant, blueberry or raspberry jam. (The raspberry is a sour fruit which contrasts with the sweetness of the base.)

The Apple Pie is a shortcrust pastry confection with a soft apple filling, is a typical English confection, which later arrived in the United States and became the American confection *par excellence*.

Together with its more tempting version, the Apple Crumble Pie, in which the apple filling is not covered by the pastry but by a layer of crunchy crumbs of flour, butter and sugar to which almonds can also be added.

SHORTCRUST PASTRY & CO
THE SWEET FOUNDATIONS

The tart is a confection consisting of a base and a filling. The former usually consists in shortcrust pastry, or short pastry or puff pastry, while the latter can range from simple jam to richer and more elaborate fillings, which often contemplate the use of custard. To prepare an excellent tart, it is important to start on the right foot with a dough worthy of the recipe, and to know perfectly how to obtain the two main fillings.

Shortcrust Pastry (*Pasta Frolla*): The Ingredients

Pasta frolla (shortcrust pastry) derives its name from the fact that, after being baked, it must be crumbly (*frolla*): able to melt in the mouth, neither hard nor elastic. A very similar pastry to this seems already to have been known in Venice around the year 1000, when cooks began to use the brown sugar coming from Egypt and Syria, but it was only towards the end of the seventeenth century that its preparation was recorded in recipe books.

Preparing shortcrust pastry is easy and requires about 20 minutes, to which you must add an hour for the dough to rest in the refrigerator.

The ingredients are: 4 cups (500g) of flour, 1 cup + 3 tbsp (300 g) of butter, 1 cup + 2 tbsp (250 g) of sugar, 2 eggs, 1 yolk, 0.12 oz (3 g; 1/5 sachet) baking powder (optional), a pinch of powdered vanilla and a pinch of salt.

To prepare cocoa shortcrust pastry, you need: 4 cups (500 g) of flour, 1 cup + 2 tbsp (285 g) of butter, 1 cup + 2 tbsp (250 g) of sugar, 1 egg, 3 yolks, 0.9 oz (25 g) of bitter cocoa, 0.12 oz (3 g; 1/5 sachet) baking powder (optional), a pinch of powdered vanilla and a pinch of salt.

If you want to make coconut shortcrust pastry, the ingredients are: 4 cups (500 g) of flour, 1 cup + 3 tbsp (300 g) of butter, 1 cup + 2 tbsp (250 g) of sugar, 1 egg, 3 yolks, 1 cup + 2 tbsp (150 g) coconut flour, the zest of half a lemon, a pinch of powdered vanilla and a pinch of salt.

For almond shortcrust pastry, you need: 4 cups (500 g) of flour, 1 cup + 7 tbsp (350 g) of butter, 1 cup + 2 tbsp (250 g) of sugar, 1 egg, 2 yolks, 5 oz (150 g) almonds, a few drops of bitter almond extract, a pinch of powdered vanilla and a pinch of salt.

For the hazelnut shortcrust pastry, you need to obtain: 4 + 3/4 cups (600 g) of flour, 1 cup + 3 tbsp (300 g) of butter, 1 cup + 2 tbsp (250 g) of sugar, 2 eggs, 7 oz (200 g) of toasted peanuts, the grated zest of half a lemon, a pinch of powdered vanilla and a pinch of salt.

Shortcrust Pastry: Method

To prepare simple cocoa or coconut shortcrust pastry, on a pastry board knead the butter softened at room temperature with the sugar, then add a pinch of salt, the yolks and the eggs. Add the sieved flour with the baking powder (optional), possibly the bitter cocoa or the grated coconut and a pinch of powdered vanilla. Knead briefly, enough to obtain an even dough. Wrap the dough in cling film and let it rest in the refrigerator for at least an hour before use.

If you want to make almond or hazelnut shortcrust pastry, you must grind the almonds or the hazelnuts in the mixer with part of the flour indicated in the recipe, stopping and starting. Then mix the powder obtained with the rest of the flour and move to the dough, as for normal shortcrust pastry.

Short Pastry: Ingredients and Method

Short pastry (*pasta brisée*) is a preparation typical of French pastries. It has a neutral taste, since it does not contain sugar, and it has a less intense yellow color than shortcrust pastry, because it does not involve the use of eggs. It is called "brisée," a French term we can translate by "broken," because first the fat is kneaded with the flour until little pieces of dough are obtained; only after-

wards do we add the quantity of cold water needed to obtain an even dough. Preparing short pastry is easy and requires about 15 minutes, to which we must add an hour's rest for the dough in the refrigerator.

The ingredients are: 8 cups (1 kg) of flour, 2 cups + 2 tbsp (500 g) of butter, about 1 cup (250 ml) of water and 4 tsp (20 g) of salt (if you wish, you can also add 1 egg, to substitute its weight in water). To prepare the short pastry, you must mix the butter with the flour and the salt, i.e. work the dough so that is becomes uneven. At this point, you can add the cold water necessary and knead (add a little at a time, in spoonfuls). After you have finished, let the dough rest in the refrigerator for an hour before using it.

Puff Pastry: Ingredients and Method

Puff pastry is a preparation based on flour, butter and water, which was created in the second half of the eighteenth century by the famous French chef Marie-Antoine Carême.

Like short pastry, it has a neutral taste, since it does not list sugar among its ingredients, and is a yellow color, because it does not use eggs.

The preparation of puff pastry is simple, but a little laborious compared to that of shortcrust and short pastry, because it consists of a precise series of moves, called "giri di pasta o di sfoglia" (rounds of dough or pastry), and requires about 2 hours.

The ingredients necessary for the so-called panetto (little loaf) are: 4 cup + 4 tbsp (1 kg) of butter and 2 cups + 4 tbsp (300 g) of type "00" flour, while for the batter you need: 5 cups + 5 tbsp (700 g) of flour for puff, 1 + 1/2 cup (370 ml) of water and 4 tsp (20 g) of salt. For the panetto, knead the butter and the flour on the pastry board, giving the dough the shape of a little loaf, and leave it to set for at least 30 minutes in the refrigerator.

For the batter, on the pastry board knead the flour, the salt and the water, then form an elastic ball without lumps and leave it to rest for at least 20 minutes in the refrigerator.

After that time has passed, roll out the batter with a rolling pin on the pastry board and place the *panetto* in the center. Wrap it, bringing the left and then the right extremities of the batter onto the *panetto*, then the upper side towards the center and the lower one. Roll out the dough to a thickness of 0.8 in (2 cm) and fold in 4.

Leave to rest in the refrigerator, covered by a cloth, for at least 20 minutes. Roll out the dough again and fold it in 4 another three times, each time in the opposite direction to the previous one, always leaving covered it to rest at least 20 minutes in the refrigerator, between one "giro" and the next.

Fruit Jam: Ingredients and Method

Fruit jam is often the most frequent tart filling: a home-made jam for an equally home-made tart. In the recipes in this book different types of jam appear: bitter cherry, raspberry, peach, apricot, mixed fruits or plum.

Preparing fruit jam at home is easy and does not require much time.

To make, for example, three 10 oz (300 g) jars of bitter cherry jam, you need 15 minutes for the preparation and 30 for cooking.

You need: 2.2 lb (1 kg) of cleaned, stoned bitter cherries (about 3.3 lb [1.5 kg] of bitter cherries to clean and stone), 3 cups + 9 tbsp (800 g) of sugar, 10 tbsp (150 ml) of water and the juice of one lemon.

To prepare the jam, put the sugar and water in a pan and bring to the boil. Add the cleaned and stoned bitter cherries and the lemon juice and cook them, continuing to stir, for at least half an hour, skimming the surface if necessary. If you prefer a smoother jam, put it through the mixer or the vegetable mill.

Check the density of the preparation, by pouring some drops onto a ceramic saucer and then tilting it: the jam must not slide off too fast, but prove viscous and quite dense. Pour the bitter cherry jam into glass jars, which have been kept up to this moment at 210°F (100°C).

Close them and turn them upside-down immediately, so that they form the vacuum necessary for increasing preservability. Keep them upside-down until they have cooled completely, then keep them in the pantry.

Custard: Ingredients and Method

Custard, the origin of which is still undecided between France and Italy, dating from the cuisine of the Medici court in Florence, is a preparation based on egg, sugar, flour and milk which is used in many tart fillings. Alone, or added to other ingredients, like fresh or dried fruit, chocolate, whipped cream.

The preparation of custard is easy and also quick: it requires about a quarter of an hour and ten minutes for cooking. Here are the ingredients: 4 egg yolks, 10 tbsp (150 g) of sugar, 3 tbsp (40 g) of type "00" flour, 2 cups (500 ml) of milk and 1 vanilla bean.

To prepare the custard, begin to heat the milk in a saucepan, with the vanilla bean cut with a knife. In the meantime, beat the yolks and the sugar in a container, then add the sieved flour and mix well. Pour a little boiling milk (from which you will have removed the cut vanilla bean) onto the eggs to melt them, then add the rest and dissolve well. Put back in the saucepan and cook until boiling. Transfer the custard into a suitable container, let it cool and then use.

16

FRUITS
AND JAM TARTS

MIXED BERRY TART

INGREDIENTS FOR 4-6 PEOPLE

9 oz (250 g) of shortcrust pastry
(see page 11)

For the filling
1/2 cup + 5 tsp (150 g) of custard
1.8 oz (50 g) of mixed fruit jam
7 in (18 cm) (circa 3.5 oz - 100 g) disk
of sponge cake

1 tbsp (15 ml) of water
2 tbsp (30 g) of sugar
4 tsp (20 ml) of Maraschino
14 oz (400 g) of assorted mixed berries
of your choice

For the finishing
powdered sugar and gelatin for desserts

PREPARATION

Line a baking pan of about 8 in (20 cm) diameter with the shortcrust pastry rolled out to a thickness of 0.12 in (3 mm). Bake it and cook before filling, placing inside it, covered with greaseproof paper, dried vegetables or rice (you can re-use them many times), at a temperature of 350°F (180°C) for about 20 minutes. Leave the bottom of the tart to cool completely before turning it out.
Boil the water and the sugar until you form a syrup, let it cool and then add the liqueur.
Spread the jam on the bottom of the tart and place on it the sponge disk, soak it with the Maraschino syrup and cover it with custard. Wash and clean the mixed berries and place them in anice formation. Complete the mixed berry tart with a dusting of powdered sugar. Alternatively, apply gelatin for desserts.

Preparation: 30' - Cooking: 20'
Difficulty: medium

EXOTIC
FRUIT TART

INGREDIENTS FOR 4-6 PEOPLE

9 oz (250 g) of coconut shortcrust pastry (see page 11)

14 oz (400 g) of assorted exotic fruit according to taste (kiwi, mango etc)

For the filling
1/2 cup (125 g) of maracuja purée
7 oz (200 g) of white chocolate
2 tbsp (30 g) of butter

For the finishing
powdered sugar or gelatin for desserts

PREPARATION

Line a baking tin of about 8 in (20 cm) diameter with the shortcrust pastry rolled out to a thickness of 0.12 in (3 mm). Bake it and cook before filling, placing inside it, covered with greaseproof paper, dried vegetables or rice (you can use them many times), at a temperature of 350°F (180°C) for about 20 minutes. Let the bottom the tart cool completely before turning it out.
In the meantime, chop up the white chocolate and put it in a bowl. Bring the maracuja in a small saucepan (obtained by blending the fruit pulp) almost to the boil and pour it onto the chocolate.
Mix well, then add the butter in pieces and mix until you obtain a smooth velvety cream.
Leave it to cool and pour it on the bottom of the tart. Leave it to set in the refrigerator for at least 30 minutes. Wash and clean the fruit, cut it into pieces, or slices according to the type, and arrange it harmoniously.
Complete the exotic fruit tart with a dusting of powdered sugar.
Alternatively, apply gelatin for desserts.

Preparation: 30' - Resting: 30'
Cooking: 20' - Difficulty: medium

ORANGE AND CHOCOLATE TART

INGREDIENTS FOR 4-6 PEOPLE

9 oz (250 g) of shortcrust pastry (see page 11)

For the orange cream
2 egg yolks
2 tbsp + 2 tsp (40 g) of sugar
6 tbsp (90 g) of orange juice
grated zest of 1 orange

2.5 oz (75 g) of white chocolate
3 tbsp (45 g) of butter
0.08 oz (2.5 g) of fish glue

For the chocolate *ganache*
1 tsp (5 g) of glucose syrup
3 tbsp + 1 tsp (50 g) of cream
1.5 oz (50 g) of dark chocolate

For the finishing
1 orange
1.5 oz (50 g) of gelatin for desserts

PREPARATION

Roll out the shortcrust pastry on a floured pastry board to a thickness of 0.12 in (3 mm). Line a baking pan of 8 in (20 cm) diameter, previously buttered and floured. Bake in the oven, placing inside, covered with greaseproof paper, dried legumes or rice, at 350°F (180°C) for 20 minutes. Turn out and leave to cool, then remove the tart from the pan. For the *ganache*, chop up the chocolate and put it in a bowl. Boil the cream with the glucose in a pan and pour it onto the chocolate. Stir until you obtain a smooth velvety cream. Pour the *ganache* into tart and put it in the refrigerator for half an hour. Chop up the white chocolate. Heat the orange juice with the zest. Beat the yolks with the sugar, then add the sugar until it boils again, beating well. Add the gelatin softened in cold water and squeezed and pour the cream on the chocolate.
Mix until it is completely dissolved. Then add the soft butter in pieces and mix well.
Complete the tart by pouring the orange cream onto the *ganache* and place in the refrigerator for 30 more minutes. Cut the orange thin and cover the surface of the tart.
Finally, brush the gelatin for desserts on top.

Preparation: 1 h - Cooling: 1 h
Cooking: 20' - Difficulty: easy

JAM
TART

INGREDIENTS FOR 4-6 PEOPLE

14 oz (400 g) of shortcrust pastry
(see page 11)

For the filling
1 cup (250 g) of jam of your choosing

PREPARATION

Line a baking pan of about 8 in (20 cm) diameter with three quarters of the shortcrust,
rolled out with a rolling pin to a thickness of 0.12 in (3 mm).
Spread a layer of jam on the bottom of the baking pan.
Cut the rest of the pastry into strips, which will be arranged in a cross pattern on the surface.
Bake at a temperature of 350°F (180°C) for about 20-25 minutes.
Leave the jam tart to cool completely before turning it out.

Preparation: 25' - Cooking: 20'-25'
Difficulty: easy

DELIGHT TART

INGREDIENTS FOR 4-6 PEOPLE

9 oz (250 g) of shortcrust pastry
(see page 11)

For the filling
3/4 cup + 4 tsp (200 g) of jam of
your choosing

For the almond paste
3.3 oz (95 g) of almonds
7.5 tbsp (115 g) of sugar
3-4 egg yolks

3 tbsp + 1 tsp (50 g) of apricot
gelatin (optional)

PREPARATION

Line a baking pan about 8 in (20 cm) in diameter with the shortcrust pastry rolled out
to a thickness of 0.12 in (3 mm). Bake it and cook before filling, placing inside it, covered with greaseproof
paper, dried legumes or rice (you can re-use them many times) in an oven at a temperature
of 350°F (180°C) for about 20 minutes. Leave the bottom of the tart to cool completely
before turning it out. Spread a layer of jam on the bottom of the baking pan.
Mill the almonds and the sugar quite finely with the cutter. Soften the paste obtained with the egg yolks.
Work the dough well: it must be just soft enough to be modeled with the pastry bag.
Decorate the surface of the tart with the almond paste, using the appropriate nozzle of the pastry bag to
create a sort of basketwork. Leave to dry for at least 12 hours, then bake in the oven at a temperature
of 440-460°F (230-240°C) for a few minutes until it acquires a slight color.
Leave it to cool and, if you wish, apply pre-heated apricot gelatin.

Preparation: 25' - Cooking: 20'+5'
Rest: 12 h - Difficulty: medium

APRICOT CREAM TART

INGREDIENTS FOR 4-6 PEOPLE

12 oz (350 g) of almond shortcrust pastry (see page 12)

For the filling
1 cup (250 g) of custard
18 oz (500 g) of fresh apricots

For the finishing
1 oz (30 g) of sliced toasted almonds
gelatin for desserts

PREPARATION

On a floured pastry board, roll out the shortcrust pastry with almond with the rolling pin to a depth of 0.12 in (3 mm). Line a baking pan of about 12 x 4 in (30 x 10 cm), buttered and floured.
Pre-cook it, placing inside, wrapped in greaseproof paper, dried legumes and rice (you can re-use them many times) in an oven at a temperature of 350°F (180°C) for about 10 minutes.
Take it out of the oven, leave it to cool for a few minutes and take out the greaseproof paper with the legumes or rice. Put the custard on the bottom of the tart and place the apricots, washed and without pits. Put back in the oven for about 20 more minutes.
Let the bottom of the tart cool completely before turning it out.
Apply gelatin for desserts to the apricot cream tart and garnish with toasted sliced almonds.

Preparation: 25' - Cooking: 30'
Difficulty: medium

STRAWBERRY TART

INGREDIENTS FOR 4-6 PEOPLE

9 oz (250 g) of shortcrust pastry
(see page 11)

4 tsp (20 g) of pistachios paste
14 oz (400 g) of strawberries

For the filling
3/4 cup + 1 tsp (185 g) of custard

For the finishing
powdered sugar

PREPARATION

Line a baking pan of about 8 in (20 cm) diameter with the shortcrust pastry
rolled out to a thickness of 0.12 in (3 mm).

Bake it and cook before filling, placing inside it, covered with greaseproof paper, dried vegetables or rice
(you can re-use them many times), at a temperature of 350°F (180°C) for about 20 minutes.
Let the bottom of the tart cool completely before turning it out.
Flavor the custard, mixing it well with the pistachios paste.
Spread the cream on the bottom of the tart.
Wash the strawberries, eliminate the green part and cut them in half.
Place them on the cream and complete the tart with a dusting of powdered sugar.

Preparation: 25' - Cooking: 20'
Difficulty: medium

FRESH FRUIT
TART

INGREDIENTS FOR 4-6 PEOPLE

9 oz (250 g) of shortcrust pastry
(see page 11)

14 oz (400 g) of fresh fruit of your
choosing

For the filling
3/4 cup + 4 tsp (200 g)
of custard

For the finishing
powdered sugar or gelatin
for desserts

PREPARATION

Line a baking pan of about 8 in (20 cm) diameter with the shortcrust pastry,
rolled out to a thickness of 0.12 in (3 mm).
Bake it and cook before filling, placing inside, covered with greaseproof paper, dried legumes or rice
(you can re-use them many times) in an oven at temperature 350°F (180°C) for about 20 minutes.
Let the bottom of the tart cool completely before turning it out,
and take out the greaseproof paper with the legumes or rice.
Place the custard on the bottom.
Wash and clean the fruit, cut it into pieces or slices according to its type and place it harmoniuosly.
Complete the fresh fruit tart with a dusting of powdered sugar.
Alternatively, to preserve it for longer, apply gelatin for desserts.

Preparation: 35' - Cooking: 20'
Difficulty: medium

NUT
TART

INGREDIENTS FOR 4 PEOPLE

9 oz (250 g) of hazelnut shortcrust pastry (see page 12)

1 oz (30 g) of pistachios
2 tsp (10 g) of type "00" flour
1 egg
1 vanilla bean

For the filling
10 tbsp (150 g) of sugar
1 oz (30 g) of hazelnuts
1 oz (30 g) of walnuts
1 oz (30 g) of almonds
1 oz (30 g) of pine nuts

For the finishing
4 oz (120 g) of assorted nuts
3 tbsp + 1 tsp (50 g) of gelatin for desserts

PREPARATION

Grind the nuts and the sugar in the food processor and add the flour.
Cut the vanilla bean with a knife and scrape the seeds, add them to the previous ingredients and add the egg. Work everything well.
Line a baking pan of about 8 in (20 cm) diameter with the hazelnut shortcrust pastry, rolled out to the thickness of 1.2 in (3 mm), then three-quarter fill it with the nut cream, previously prepared, and bake it at 350°F (180°C) for about 25 minutes.
Let the tart cool, turn it out and decorate it with the assorted nuts.
Finally, apply the gelatin for desserts to the nuts.

Preparation: 35' - Cooking: 25'
Difficulty: easy

APPLE TART

INGREDIENTS FOR 4-6 PEOPLE

9 oz (250 g) of shortcrust pastry
(see page 11)

4 tsp (20 g) of sugar

For the filling
18 oz (500 g) of apples

For the finishing
4 tbsp (60 g) of gelatin
for desserts

PREPARATION

Line a baking pan of about 8 in (20 cm) diameter with the shortcrust pastry
rolled out to a thickness of 0.12 in (3 mm).
Peel the apples and throw away the core, cut them in half and cut them
into 0.08-0.12 in (2-3 mm) thick slices. Place the apple slices in an orderly way,
overlapping them slightly, on the bottom of the baking pan. Dust them with the sugar.
Bake at a temperature of 350°F (180°C) for about 20-25 minutes.
Leave the tart to cool completely before turning it out.
Apply gelatin for desserts, heated in a small saucepan, to the apple tart.

Preparation: 30' - Cooking: 20'-25'
Difficulty: easy

PEAR TART
WITH GRAPPA

INGREDIENTS FOR 4-6 PEOPLE

12 oz (350 g) of shortcrust pastry
(see page 11)

2 tbsp + 3 tsp (40 g) of cornstarch
5 tsp (25 ml) of *Grappa*

For the filling
1 1/4 lb (600 g) of pears
7 tbsp (100 g) of sugar

For the finishing
gelatin for desserts
powdered sugar

PREPARATION

Peel the pears, throw away the core and cut them into small cubes of sides about 0.4 in (1 cm).
Moisten with the Grappa and let them take the flavor for at least 10 minutes.
In the meantime, cover a baking pan of about 8 in (20 cm) diameter with three quarters of the shortcrust
pastry, rolled out to a thickness of 0.12 in (3 mm).
Mix the sugar and the starch in a bowl. Mix the pears with the mixture of sugar and starch.
Distribute the pear fillling on the bottom of the shortcrust in the baking pan,
then cover with the rest of the pastry cut into strips.
Bake in an oven at temperature 350°F (180°C) for about 35 minutes.
Take out of the oven and leave the pear tart with Grappa to cool completely, before turning it out.
Dust with powdered sugar and put a little gelatin for desserts on the pears,
between the strips of shortcrust pastry.

Preparation: 30' - Cooking: 35'
Difficulty: easy

PEAR AND CHOCOLATE TART

INGREDIENTS FOR 4-6 PEOPLE

9 oz (250 g) of shortcrust pastry
(see page 11)

For the filling
1 egg + 2 yolks
1/2 cup + 2 tsp (120 g) of sugar
4 tsp (20 g) of almonds flour
5 tsp (20 g) of type "00" flour
2 tsp (10 g) of cocoa

1/2 cup + 3 tbsp (165 ml) of milk
7 tbsp (100 ml) of cream
1/2 vanilla bean
9 oz (250 g) of drained pears in
syrup

For the finishing
3 tbsp + 1 tsp (50 g) of gelatin for
desserts

PREPARATION

In a container beat the egg and yolks with the sugar, add the sieved flour with cocoa
and the powdered almonds. Add the milk, boiled separately with the cream, and the half cut vanilla bean,
and cook like a normal cream. Leave to cool.
In the meantime, roll out the shortcrust pastry with a rolling pin on a floured pastry board
to a thickness of 0.12 in (3 mm). Line a baking pan of about 8 in (20 cm) in diameter.
Cut the half drained pears in syrup into slices of 0.12-0.16 in (3-4 mm) thickness
and place them on the bottom of the tart.
Pour the mixture previously obtained, bake at a temperature of 320°F (160°C) for about 30 minutes.
Turn out the pear and chocolate tart and cool. As soon as the tart is cool,
gloss the pears with a little gelatin for desserts.

Preparation: 30' - Cooking: 30'
Difficulty: easy

LINZER TART

INGREDIENTS FOR 4-6 PEOPLE

For the pastry (see page 11)
6 tbsp (85 g) of butter
1/2 cup (65 g) of powdered sugar
1 egg
1 cup + 3 tbsp (165 g) of type "00" flour
4 tbsp (50 g) of almond flour
powdered vanilla
0.04 oz (1 g) of powdered cinnamon

1/4 tsp (1 g) of baking powder
a pinch of salt

For the filling
1 cup (250 g) of raspberry jam

For the finishing
raspberry gelatin (seedless)

PREPARATION

Knead the soft butter and the powdered sugar, then add a pinch of salt and the egg.
Add the sieved flour with the baking powder (optional), a pinch of powdered vanilla and the cinnamon,
mix the almonds flour and knead everything briefly, just enough to obtain an even pastry.
Wrap in film and leave in the refrigerator for at least two hours before use.
Line a baking tin of about 8 in (20 cm) diameter with two thirds of the shortcrust pastry rolled out
to a thickness of 0.12 in (3 mm). Spread a layer of jam on the bottom of the baking tin.
Cut the rest of the shortcrust pastry into strips, which will then be placed criss-cross on the surface.
Bake in an oven at a temperature of 350°F (180°C) for about 20-25 minutes.
Leave the jam tart to cool completely before turning it out.
If you wish, apply raspberry gelatin (without seeds) to the Linzer tart.

Preparation: 25' - Rest: 2 h
Cooking: 20'-25' - Difficulty: easy

THREE-JAM MINI TARTS

INGREDIENTS FOR 4-6 PEOPLE

12 oz (350 g) of shortcrust pastry (see page 11)

For the filling
3/4 cup (180 g) of three types of jam of your choice

For the finishing
powdered sugar

PREPARATION

Roll out the shortcrust pastry on a floured pastry board to a thickness of 0.12 in (3 mm).
Make 8 circles with a dough cutter of about 4 in (10 cm) diameter.
In half of these make three holes with small dough cutters in your chosen form (square, circle, triangle, etc).
Bake them in the oven at a temperature of 350°F (180°C) for about 15-20 minutes.
Leave them to cool completely, then put every full circle together with a holed one,
after having spread the edges with a thin veil of jam.
Dust the tarts with the powdered sugar and pour the various jams into the holes (possibly heated
in a small pan if very dense).

Preparation: 25' - Cooking: 15'-20'
Difficulty: easy

PINEAPPLE UPSIDE-DOWN TART

INGREDIENTS FOR 4-6 PEOPLE

7 oz (200 g) of shortcrust pastry (see page 11)

18 oz (500 g) of pineapple (about 1/2 pineapple)
1/2 cup + 3 tbsp (160 g) of sugar
3 tbsp (40 g) of butter
1 egg yolk
3 tbsp + 1 tsp (50 g) of milk

6.5 tbsp (85 g) of type "00" flour
1 tsp (4 g) of baking powder
a pinch of salt
lemon zest
1/2 vanilla bean

For the finishing
gelatin for desserts

PREPARATION

Caramelize 1/2 cup (120 g) of sugar in a small saucepan and pour it onto the bottom of the baking pan.
Peel the pineapple and discard the center.
Make slices about 0.4 in (1 cm) thick and cut them to fit them to the baking tin bottom.
Mix, very well, the soft butter and the remaining 3 tbsp (40 g of sugar) in a basin.
Add the yolk, the milk, the salt, a grating of lemon zest and the beans of the vanilla cut and scraped with the point of a knife. Add the sieved flour with the baking powder. Pour this mixture onto the pineapple.
Roll out the shortcrust pastry on a pastry board with a rolling pin to a thickness of 0.12 in (3 mm).
Cut out a disk with the same diameter of the baking tin, pierce it with a fork and place it on the tart filling.
Bake for about 35 minutes at 350°F (180°C).
Turn out the tart upside-down on a serving dish, when it is completely cold
(to make this easier, hold the baking tin for a few moments over the gas),
and then apply gelatin for desserts to the surface.

Preparation: 20' - Cooking: 35'
Difficulty: easy

APPLE UPSIDE-DOWN CAKE

INGREDIENTS FOR 4-6 PEOPLE

7 oz (200 g) of short pastry (see page 11) or puff pastry (see page 13)

For the filling
2.6 lb (1.2 kg) of apples
1/2 cup + 2 tbsp (150 g) of sugar

3 tbsp (40 g) of butter

For the finishing
gelatin for desserts

PREPARATION

Caramelize 1/2 cup (120 g) of sugar in a small saucepan and pour it on the bottom of the baking tin.
Peel the apples, discarding the core, and cut them in four.
Place them like spokes, close together, in the tin and on the surface place the butter
in small pieces and the rest of the sugar.
Bake for about 20 minutes at a temperature of 350°F (180°C).
Leave to cool and cover with a disk of short pastry (or puff pastry) pierced with a fork.
Bake for another 30 minutes.
When the tart is completely cold, turn it out, turning it upside-down (to make this easier,
hold the baking tin for a few moments over the gas) on a serving
dish and apply gelatin for desserts to the surface.

Preparation: 20' - Cooking: 50'
Difficulty: easy

UPSIDE-DOWN
PEAR CAKE
WITH RED WINE

INGREDIENTS FOR 4-6 PEOPLE

7 oz (200 g) of short pastry (see
page 11) or puff pastry (see page 13)

2.2 lb (1 kg) of pears
2 cup (500 ml) of red wine
1 cup (220 g) of sugar

4 tsp (20 g) butter
1-2 cloves
cinnamon

For the finishing
gelatin for desserts

PREPARATION

Peel the pears, cut them in half, remove the core with a corer and place them
in a tall narrow saucepan so that they are covered by the red wine.
Add 1/2 cup (110 g) sugar, 1-2 cloves and a piece of cinnamon.
Cook on a low flame for 15-20 minutes as long as the pears are still quite firm (test with a toothpick),
remembering that the cooking time also depends on the variety of pear used.
Leave to cool in the pan.
Caramelize 1/2 cup (110 g) sugar in a small saucepan and pour it onto the bottom of the baking pan.
Drain the pears well and place them in the baking pan, with the cut part downwards.
Add the butter in pieces and cover with a disk of short pastry (or puff pastry) pierced with a fork.
Bake in the oven at temperature 350°F (180°C) for 30 minutes.
When the tart is completely cold, turn it upside-down (to make this easier,
move the baking pan for a few moments over the flame)
on a serving dish and then apply gelatin for desserts to the surface.

Preparation: 20' - Cooking: 45'-50'
Difficulty: easy

TARTS AND GOURMET CAKES

GRANDMOTHER'S PINE NUT TART

INGREDIENTS FOR 4-6 PEOPLE

9 oz (250 g) of shortcrust pastry
(see page 11)

For the filling
5 tbsp (70 g) of custard
3 tbsp + 1 tsp (50 g) of butter
3 tbsp + 1 tsp (50 g) of sugar
0.70 oz (20 g) of pine nuts

1 oz (30 g) of almonds
1 tbsp (10 g) of type "00" flour
2 tsp (10 ml) of rum
1 egg

For the finishing
1.70 oz (50 g) of pine nuts
powdered sugar

PREPARATION

Put the almonds, pine nuts and sugar into a food mixer and pulse till you achieve a powder consistency.
In a mixing bowl, work the butter and the powder obtained at room temperature,
add the flour and lastly the egg. Add the custard and the rum.
Line a baking pan of about 8 in (20 cm) diameter with the shortcrust pastry rolled out to the thickness
of 0.12 in (3 mm), then three quarter fill it with the paste obtained.
Cover with the pine nuts, dust lightly with powdered sugar and bake in the oven
at temperature 350°F (180°C) for about 25 minutes.
Leave the grandmother's pine-nut tart to cool, turn it out and dust again with powdered sugar.

Preparation: 30' - Cooking: 25'
Difficulty: medium

CARAMEL
TART

INGREDIENTS FOR 4-6 PEOPLE

9 oz (250 g) of hazelnut
shortcrust pastry (see page 12)

For the caramel
10 tbsp (150 g) of sugar
2 tbsp (30 g) of butter
10 tbsp (150 g) of cream
a pinch of salt

For the chocolate *ganache*
1 tsp (5 g) of glucose syrup
3 tbsp + 1 tsp (50 g) of cream
2.8 oz (80 g) of milk
chocolate

**For the hazelnuts glazed
with sugar**
4 oz (125 g) of toasted and
peeled hazelnuts
7 tbsp (100 g) of sugar
2 tbsp (30 ml) of water

PREPARATION

Roll the shortcrust pastry out on a floured pastry board to a thickness of 0.12 in (3 mm). Line a baking pan of
6 in (15 cm) sides, previously buttered and floured. Bake it and cook before filling, placing inside it, covered
with greaseproof paper, dried legumes or rice, at 350°F (180°C) for about 20 minutes. Turn out and leave to
cool, then remove the tart from the pan. For the caramel, caramelize the sugar in a small saucepan. As soon
as becomes yellow, add the cream, previously heated, and the butter in pieces. Add a pinch of salt, mix well
until the caramel is smooth and even. Leave it to cool and pour into the bottom of the tart. Leave it to set
for at least half an hour. For the *ganache*, chop up the chocolate and put it in a bowl. Boil the cream in a pan
with the glucose and pour it onto the chocolate. Mix well, until you obtain a smooth, velvety cream.
Pour the *ganache* into the tart and put it in the refrigerator for at least half an hour.
For the hazelnuts, bring the sugar and water in a small saucepan to the boil.
Add the hazelnuts and cook, stirring, until the sugar is crystallized.
Pour them onto a baking tin to let them cool. Decorate the tart with the hazelnuts glazed.

Preparation: 1 h - Cooking: 18'-20'
Cooling: 1 h - Difficulty: medium

TART WITH CHOCOLATE AND RASPBERRIES

INGREDIENTS FOR 4-6 PEOPLE

9 oz (250 g) of cocoa shortcrust pastry (see page 11)

For the filling
3 tbsp + 1 tsp (50 g) of raspberry jam

For the white chocolate *ganache*
7 tbsp (100 ml) of cream
2 tsp (10 g) of glucose syrup
9 oz (250 g) of white chocolate

For the dark chocolate *ganache*
2 tsp (10 ml) of cream
0.7 oz (20 g) of dark chocolate

For the finishing
9 oz (250 g) of fresh raspberries
powdered sugar

PREPARATION

Roll the shortcrust pastry with cocoa with a rolling pin on a floured pastry board to the thickness of 0.12 in (3 mm). Line a buttered and floured baking pan of 8 in (20 cm) diameter.
Spread with the raspberry jam and bake in oven at 350°F for 18-20 minutes.
Turn out and let cool, then remove the tart from the pan. For the white chocolate *ganache*, chop up the chocolate and put it in a bowl. Boil the cream in a small saucepan with the glucose and pour it onto the chocolate. Mix well, until you obtain a smooth and velvet cream. Do the same with the dark chocolate.
Let it cool and pour the white *ganache* into the tart up to the level of the edge. With a pastry bag filled with dark chocolate *ganache* draw lines or a spiral on the surface and streak them with the point of a knife.
Garnish with fresh raspberries which you have previously washed and dried, and put the tart to set for at least an hour in the refrigerator.
Dust with the edge of the tart with powdered sugar before serving.

Preparation: 45' - Cooking: 18'-20'
Cooling: 1 h - Difficulty: medium

ORANGE TART

INGREDIENTS FOR 4-6 PEOPLE

9 oz (250 g) of cocoa
shortcrust pastry
(see page 11)

5 oranges
2 tbsp + 2 tsp (40 g) of sugar
2 tbsp (25 g) of cornstarch

For the orange paste
10 tbsp (150 ml) of juice
(obtained from peeling the 5
oranges)
1 egg yolk
2 tbsp + 2 tsp (40 g) of sugar
2 tsp (10 g) of type "00" flour
1 gelatin leaf

For the Italian meringue
1 egg white
4 tbsp + 1 tsp (65 g) of sugar
1 tbsp (15 ml) of water

For the finishing
chopped pistachios
chocolate

PREPARATION

Line a baking pan of 8 in (20 cm) diameter, buttered and floured, with the shortcrust pastry rolled out to thickness of 0.12 in (3 mm). Peel the oranges with a sharp knife, removing zest and white skin. You obtain 14 oz (400 g) of segments. Squeeze the remaining and preserve the juice. Mix sugar and cornstarch and pour them onto the orange segments, mix into a baking pan and bake it at 350°F (180°C) for 25 minutes. Leave the bottom of the tart to cool before turning it out. Heat 10 tbsp (150 ml) of orange juice in a small saucepan. Beat the yolk with the sugar, then add the sieved flour. Dilute with the juice and cook until it boils again, beating well. Place the softened gelatin in cold water, squeezed and mix until it dissolves completely. For the Italian meringue, in a small saucepan begin to cook 4 tbsp (55 g) of sugar with the water. In the meantime, whip the egg whites with 2 tsp (10 g) of sugar. When the mixture has reached 250°F (120°C), drizzle into the whipped egg whites and beat until cooling. Add the meringue to the orange paste and pour it on the cold tart, leveling off with a spatula. Decorate with pistachios and chocolate. Leave to cool for an hour in the refrigerator before serving.

Preparation: 1 h - Cooking: 20'
Rest: 1 h - Difficulty: easy

BLACK FOREST
CHERRY TART

INGREDIENTS FOR 4-6 PEOPLE

9 oz (250 g) of cocoa
shortcrust pastry
(see page 11)

For the filling
12 oz (350 g) of frozen
cherries, thawed and
stoned
4 tbsp + 2 tsp (70 g) of
sugar

3 tbsp (40 g) of cornstarch
juice of 1/2 lemon

For the *panna cotta* with cherries
2 oz (65 g) of frozen
cherries, thawed and
stoned
4 tbsp (60 g) of sugar
2 tsp (8 g) of cornstarch

5-6 drops of lemon juice
1/2 cup (125 ml) of cream
0.9 oz (2.5 g) of fish glue

For the finishing
black cherries in syrup,
drained
garnishes in chocolate

PREPARATION

Roll out the cocoa shortcrust pastry on a pastry board with a rolling pin to a thickness of 0.12 in (3 mm).
Line a baking pan 9 in (20 cm) in diameter, previously buttered and floured.
Mix the ingredients of the filling and fill the tart. Bake in an oven at a temperature of 340°F (170°C)
for about 18-20 minutes. Leave to cool.
For the disk of *panna cotta* with cherries, in a small saucepan mix the cherries, the sugar, the cornstarch
and the lemon juice and boil for 1-2 minutes. Add the cream and bring everything to the boil.
Add the fish glue, softened in cold water, and squeezed and dissolve it well.
Pour the *panna cotta* into a round mold of smaller diameter than that of the tart.
Leave in the refrigerator for two hours. Turn out the *panna cotta*, place it on the tart and garnish
as you wish with the drained stoned black cherries in syrup and decorate in chocolate.

Preparation: 1 h - Cooking: 18'-20'
Rest: 2 h - Difficulty: medium

CREMA COTTA TART

INGREDIENTS FOR 4-6 PEOPLE

12 oz (350 g) of shortcrust pastry (see page 11)

For the filling
1/2 cup (125 ml) of milk
2 tbsp (30 g) of semolina
1 tbsp + 2 tsp (25 g) of sugar
2 egg yolks
1.4 oz (40 g) of raisins

a pinch of salt
10 tbsp (150 g) of custard
zest of 1/2 lemon
1/2 vanilla bean

For the finishing
2 tbsp (30 g) of gelatine for desserts
powdered sugar

PREPARATION

Start to boil the milk in a small saucepan with the lemon zest (only the yellow part), the vanilla, cut and scraped with the point of a knife, and the salt. When it boils, take out the vanilla and the lemon zest, then drizzle in the semolina and cook for 3-4 minutes on a low flame. Take it off the flame and add the yolks and the raisins, which have softened in lukewarm water for about 10 minutes. Leave to cool and add the custard. Lie a baking pan of about 8 in (20 cm) diameter with the shortcrust pastry rolled out to a thickness of 0.12 in (3 mm). Spread the bottom of the baking pan with the semolina cream.
Cut little strips with the rest of the shortcrust and place them on the surface. Bake in an oven at temperature 350°F (180°C) for about 20-25 minutes. Leave the tart to cool completely before turning it out. Cut little strips of paper and cover part of the tart, dust the tart with *crema cotta* with powdered sugar, then remove the little strips carefully. Brush the remaining parts without sugar with gelatin for desserts, previously heated in a small saucepan.

Preparation: 30' - Cooking: 20'-25'
Difficulty: easy

CHOCOLATE CREAM TART

INGREDIENTS FOR 4-6 PEOPLE

9 oz (250 g) of cocoa shortcrust
pastry (see page 11)

3 tbsp (45 g) of cornstarch
2 cups (500 ml) of milk

For the filling
3 eggs
10 tbsp (150 g) of sugar
3 tbsp (40 g) of bitter cocoa

For the finishing
3/4 cup + 1 tbsp (200 g) of whipped
sugared cream

PREPARATION

Line a baking tin of about 8 in (20 cm) diameter with the shortcrust pastry with cocoa,
rolled out to a thickness of 0.12 in (3 mm).
Boil the milk in a small saucepan; in the meantime, beat the 3 eggs with the sugar,
then add the sieved cornstarch and the cocoa.
Add the boiling milk little by little, mix well, then cook for 1-2 minutes, mixing with a whisk.
Pour immediately into the baking tin and bake for about 35-40 minutes
at temperature 350°F (180°C) until the filling is quite firm.
Let the chocolate cream tart cool completely before turning it out.
Complete the chocolate cream tart with whipped cream applied with a pastry bag with a rigid nozzle.

Preparation: 30' - Cooking: 35'-40'
Difficulty: easy

TART
WITH CHESTNUT CREAM

INGREDIENTS FOR 4-6 PEOPLE

9 oz (250 g) of cocoa shortcrust
pastry (see page 11)

5 tbsp (75 g) of cream
1 leaf fish glue

For the filling
1 cup + 3 tbsp (300 g) of non-
sugared chestnut cream
1 cup + 1 tbsp (125 g) of powdered
sugar
2 tbsp (25 g) of cocoa
1 tsp (5 ml) of rum

For the finishing
chestnuts in syrup
little meringues
cocoa
powdered sugar

PREPARATION
Line a baking pan of about 8 in (20 cm) diameter with the shortcrust pastry with cocoa,
rolled out to a thickness of 0.12 in (3 mm).
Bake it and cook before filling, placing inside, covered with greaseproof paper, dried legumes or rice
(you can re-use them many times), at a temperature of 350°F (180°C) for about 20 minutes.
Leave to cool the bottom of the tart completely before turning it out.
Work very well the chestnut cream with the sieved powdered sugar and cocoa, until it is smooth and even;
then add the partially whipped cream, the rum and the fish glue, which has previously been softened in cold
water and wrung. Distribute the resulting cream on the bottom of the pre-cooked shortcrust using a pastry
bag with a big smooth nozzle (or, alternatively, simply spreading it with a spatula).
Decorate the tart with chestnuts and little meringues and a dusting
of cocoa and powdered sugar.

Preparation: 40' - Cooking: 20'
Difficulty: medium

BANANA AND CHOCOLATE TART WITH RUM

INGREDIENTS FOR 4-6 PEOPLE

9 oz (250 g) of cocoa shortcrust pastry (see page 11)

For the filling
18 oz (500 g) of bananas
1/2 cup (100 g) of brown sugar
3 tbsp + 1 tsp (50 ml) of rum

For the *ganache*
1 cup + 1 tbsp (270 g) of cream
2 tbsp + 1 tsp (35 ml) of glucose syrup
10 oz (300 g) of dark chocolate
6 oz (180 g) of milk chocolate

5 tbsp (70 g) of butter
2 tbsp + 1 tsp (35 ml) of rum

For the finishing
chocolate curls
powdered sugar

PREPARATION

For the *ganache*, chop up the chocolates and put them in a bowl. In a small saucepan, boil the cream with the glucose syrup and pour it, boiling, onto the chocolate. Mix carefully with a soft spatula (do not use the whisk because too much air would come in) until you obtain a smooth, velvety cream. Add the soft butter in small pieces and, finally, the rum. Fill to the height of 0.8 in (2 cm) a mold of slightly smaller diameter to that of the baking pan which will be used and frozen for 2 hours. Put on one side the remaining *ganache*. Line a baking pan of about 8 in (20 cm) with the shortcrust pastry rolled out to 0.12 in (3 mm). Bake at 350°F (180°C) for 15-20 minutes. In a pan, melt the sugar on a medium flame, add the sliced bananas and, when they begin to caramelize, flambé them with the rum. Pour them on the bottom of the shortcrust pastry, which has been previously cooked. Turn out the disk of frozen *ganache* and place it in the center of the tart thus filled. Let it thaw. In the meantime, beat the remaining *ganache* with a whisk and create a border around the chocolate disk with a pastry nag with nozzle. Complete with curls of chocolate and a dusting of powdered sugar.

Preparation: 1 h - Freezing: 2 h
Cooking: 15'-20' - Difficulty: high

RICOTTA TART
WITH DARK CHOCOLATE GANACHE

INGREDIENTS FOR 4-6 PEOPLE

12 oz (350 g) of shortcrust pastry
(see page 11)

a pinch of salt
a pinch of powdered vanilla

For the filling
1/2 cup + 2 tbsp (150 g) of ricotta
2 tbsp (30 g) of butter
2 tbsp + 1 tsp (35 g) of sugar
2 tsp (10 g) of type "00" flour

For the dark chocolate *ganache*
5 tbsp (75 ml) of cream
2 tsp (8 g) of glucose syrup
5 oz (150 g) of dark chocolate

PREPARATION

Roll out the shortcrust pastry with a rolling pin on a floured pastry board to a thickness of 0.12 in (3 mm).
Line a baking pan about 12 x 5 in (30 x 12 cm), buttered and floured.
Sieve the ricotta, then work it in a container with the sugar, the pinch of salt and the pinch of vanilla.
Add the sieved flour, then the melted warm butter.
Work everything well, then spread on the bottom of the tart and bake in an oven
at temperature 340°F (170°C) for about 25-30 minutes.
Turn out and leave to cool, then remove the tart from the pan.
For the chocolate *ganache*, chop up the dark chocolate and put it in a bowl. Boil the cream
and the glucose syrup in a small pan and pour it onto the chocolate. Mix well, until you obtain a smooth,
velvety cream. Let it cool and then pour it onto the tart up to the edge.
Put the tart with ricotta and dark chocolate to set in the refrigerator for at least an hour.
Decorate to taste.

Preparation: 45' - Cooking: 25'-30'
Rest: 1 h - Difficulty: medium

CREAMY PISTACHIO TART

INGREDIENTS FOR 4-6 PEOPLE

9 oz (250 g) of shortcrust pastry (see page 11)

For the filling
3 tbsp + 1 tsp (50 g) of raspberry jam

For the *panna cotta* with pistachios
3/4 cup + 4 tsp (200 ml) of cream
8 tsp (40 g) of sugar
0.2 oz (5 g) of fish glue
7 tsp (35 g) of pistachios paste

For the Italian meringue
2 whites of egg
1/2 cup (125 g) of sugar
2 tbsp (30 ml) of water

PREPARATION

For the *panna cotta*, mix the cream and the sugar in a small saucepan and bring to the boil.
Add the fish glue, softened in cold water and wrung, and squeezed of all liquids and dissolved.
Dissolve the pistachios paste in the boiling liquid. Pour the *panna cotta* into a round mold of diameter smaller than that of the tart. Leave in the refrigerator for 2 hours.
Line a baking pan of about 8 in (20 cm) diameter with the shortcrust pastry to a thickness of 0.12 in (3 mm).
Bake it and cook before filling, placing inside it, covered with greaseproof paper, dried legumes and rice, in an oven at 350°F (180°C) for about 20 minutes. Let the bottom of the tart cool before turning it out.
Spread the raspberry jam on the bottom of the tart, turn out the *panna cotta* and place it on the tart.
For the Italian meringue, cook in a small saucepan, preferably copper, the 7 tbsp (110 g) of sugar with the water. In the meantime, beat the whites of egg with the 1 tbsp (15 g) of sugar.
When it has reached 250°F (120°C), pour it slowly into the beaten egg whites and beat until they cool. Decorate the tart with the meringue using a pastry bag and light it with the appropriate device.

Preparation: 1 h - Cooking: 20'
Rest: 2 h - Difficulty: medium

MANGO AND COCONUT TART

INGREDIENTS FOR 4-6 PEOPLE

9 oz (250 g) of coconut shortcrust pastry (see page 11)

For the filling
a mango of about 18 oz (500 g)
3 tbsp +1 tsp (50 g) of sugar
some drops of lemon juice

4.5 tbsp (65 g) of butter
4 tbsp + 1 tsp (65 g) of sugar
1 egg
1 yolk
2 tbsp (30 ml) of milk
5 tbsp (65 g) of type "00" flour
1/2 vanilla bean

1/2 tsp (2 g) of baking powder
5 tbsp (65 g) of coconut flour
salt

For the finishing
coconut flour
gelatin for desserts

PREPARATION

Line a baking pan of about 8 in (20 cm) diameter with shortcrust pastry rolled out to a thickness of 0.12 in (3 mm). Clean the mango, cut it into slices, put it in a pan with 3 tbsp and 1 tsp (50 g) of sugar and some drops of lemon. Cook on a low gas for about 10 minutes.
In the meantime, work well the soft butter and 4 tbsp and 1 tsp (65 g) of sugar.
Add the egg and the yolk, then the milk. With the tip of a knife, open up the half vanilla bean and scrape the seeds. Add them to the preparation. Then add the sieved flour with the baking powder, mixed with a pinch of salt and with the coconut flour. First pour the cooked mango and then coconut mixture into the baking pan and bake in the oven at a temperature of 350°F (180°C) for about 30 minutes.
Leave the mango and coconut tart to cool completely before turning it out.
Apply gelatin for desserts to the surface and stick on some of the coconut flour.

Preparation: 50' - Cooking: 30'
Difficulty: medium

TART WITH MANGO, MARACUJA AND PINK GRAPEFRUIT

INGREDIENTS FOR 4-6 PEOPLE

9 oz (250 g) of shortcrust pastry (see page 11)

For the filling
a mango of about 14 oz (400 g)
5 tbsp (70 g) of sugar

2.5 tbsp (35 g) of cornstarch
juice of 1/2 lemon
1/2 cup (125 g) of maracuja purée
1 egg yolk
1 leaf of gelatin

For Italian meringue
2 whites of egg
8 tbsp (125 g) of sugar
2 tbsp (30) ml of water

For the finishing
2 pink grapefruit
gelatin for desserts

PREPARATION

Line a baking pan of about 8 in (20 cm) diameter with the shortcrust pastry to a thickness of 0.12 in (3 mm).
Clean the mango, cut it into cubes and moisten it with the lemon juice. Mix 3 tbsp and 1 tsp (50 g)
of sugar and cornstarch and pour them onto the mango, mix them, pour it all into
a baking pan and bake at 350°F (180°C) for 25 minutes. Let the tart cool before turning it out. In the
meantime, heat the maracuja purée in a small frying pan. Beat the white of egg and the rest of the sugar,
then combine with the purée and cook until it boils again, beating well.
Add the gelatin softened in cold water and wrung and mix until it is completely dissolved.
For the preparation of the Italian meringue, see the recipe "Creamy pistachios tart" on page 74.
Add the maracuja cream meringue and place it on the cold tart. Let it set for half an hour in the freezer,
and then flame the cream with the appropriate device. Peel the grapefruit with a sharp knife,
removing not only the peel but the white skin. Separate the segments, passing a knife between
the segment and the membrane that separates it from the others.
Surround it with grapefruit segments and apply gelatin for desserts.

Preparation: 1 h - Cooling: 30'
Cooking: 25' - Difficulty: high

PECAN NUT TART

INGREDIENTS FOR 4-6 PEOPLE

9 oz (250 g) of shortcrust pastry (see page 11)

For the caramel
5 tbsp (75 g) of sugar
1 tbsp (15 g) of butter
5 tbsp (75 ml) of cream

For the filling
7 tbsp (100 g) of butter
7 tbsp (100 g) of sugar
4 tbsp (50 g) of type "00" flour
2 tbsp (30 g) of potato starch
2 oz (60 g) of pecans
1 egg + 3 yolks

1/2 tsp (2 g) of baking powder
1 oz (30 g) of dark chocolate

For the finishing
3 oz (90 g) of pecans
powdered sugar

PREPARATION

Roll out the shortcrust pastry with a rolling pin on a floured pastry board to a thickness of 0.12 in (3 mm).
Line a buttered and floured baking pan 8 in (20 cm) in diameter.
Caramelize the sugar in a small saucepan and, as soon as it reaches a yellow color, add the cream,
heated separately, and the butter in pieces, then mix well, moving the saucepan
until the caramel is very smooth and even. Leave to cool and pour into the bottom of the shortcrust.
Grind the nuts finely with a little flour in a mixer, stopping and starting.
Work the soft butter and the sugar well, then add the egg and the yolks a little at a time.
Add the nut powder, the melted chocolate and lastly the sifted flour with the potato starch
and the baking powder. Fill three quarters of the baking pan and cover the surface with
the pecan nut kernels. Dust with powdered sugar and bake in an oven
at 350°F (180°C) for about 30 minutes.

Preparation: 45' - Cooking: 30'
Difficulty: medium

PEACH AND ALMOND TART

INGREDIENTS FOR 4-6 PEOPLE

14 oz (400 g) of almond
shortcrust pastry (see page 12)

For the filling
1 egg + 2 yolks
2 tbsp + 1 tsp (35 g) of sugar
2 tbsp (25 g) of type "00" flour
2 tsp (8 g) of potato starch
0.7 oz (20 g) of almonds

0.17 oz (5 g) of bitter almonds
1 tbsp (17 g) of butter
3 tbsp (50 g) of peach jam
2 peaches (fresh or in syrup)
Amaretto grain
grain or sliced almonds

For the finishing
powdered sugar

82

PREPARATION

Line a baking pan with about 8 in (20 cm) diameter with three quarters of the shortcrust pastry
with almonds, roll out to a thickness of 0.12 in (3 mm), then spread a layer of jam on it,
arrange sliced fresh peaches or peaches in syrup and then spread with the *Amaretto* grain.
Whip the egg, the yolks and the sugar, after you have heated everything lightly in a saucepan, always mixing
with a whisk. In the meantime, grind the almonds and the bitter almonds in the cutter,
mix them with flour and potato starch, and then put everything in the whipped eggs and sugar.
Finally, add the melted butter. Fill the baking pan, spread with grain or sliced almonds.
On top, criss-cross strips of shortcrust pastry and bake in an oven at temperature 350°F (180°C)
for about 35 minutes. Leave the peach and almond tart to cool completely before turning it out.
Dust the peach and almond tart with powdered sugar.

Preparation: 40' - Cooking: 35'
Difficulty: high

RICOTTA TART
WITH LIME

INGREDIENTS FOR 4-6 PEOPLE

12 oz (350 g) of shortcrust pastry
(see page 11)

For the filling
1 cup + 2 tbsp (250 g) of ricotta
3 tbsp + 1 tsp (50 g) of butter
4 tbsp + 1 tsp (65 g) of sugar

1 tbsp (15 g) of type "00" flour
2 oz (65 g) of raisins
a pinch of salt
1 lime

For the finishing
gelatin for desserts

PREPARATION

Sieve the ricotta, then work it carefully with the sugar.
Add in sequence, mixing well, the melted butter, the flour, the juice and the grated lime zest,
a pinch of salt and, lastly, the raisins softened for a few minutes in lukewarm water and squeezed.
Line a baking pan of 7-8 in (18-20 cm) diameter with three quarters of the shortcrust pastry,
rolled out to a thickness of 0.12 in (3 mm). Fill with the ricotta mixture and level well.
Make strips from the remaining shortcrust, garnish the tart and bake it in the oven at a temperature
of 350°F (180°C) for about 30 minutes.
Leave the ricotta tart with lime to cool completely before turning it out.
Apply gelatin for desserts to the surface.

Preparation: 20' - Cooking: 30'
Difficulty: medium

FRANGIPANE TART
WITH BLACK CHERRIES

INGREDIENTS FOR 4-6 PEOPLE

7 oz (200 g) of almond
shortcrust pastry
(see page 12)
5 tbsp (70 g) of black cherry
jam
4 tbsp (60 g) of drained
black cherries in syrup

For the filling
3 tbsp + 1 tsp (50 g) of butter
4 tbsp (60 g) of sugar
3 tbsp (40 g) of type "00"
flour
1.4 oz (40 g) of almonds
0.17 oz (5 g) of bitter almonds

2 egg + 1 yolk
0.07 oz (2 g) of ammonia
bicarbonate for sweets

For the finishing
powdered sugar
almonds

PREPARATION

Line a baking pan of about 8 in (20 cm) diameter with shortcrust pastry with almonds,
rolled out to a thickness of 0.08-0.12 in (2-3 mm), then spread black cherry jam on the bottom
and arrange some drained black cherries in syrup.
Grind the almonds and bitter almonds finely with a mixer, stopping and starting.
Mix in the planetary, with flat beater, the butter and the almond powder.
Add the 3 yolks a little at a time, the ammonium bicarbonate and, lastly, the 2 whites of egg whipped
with sugar. Three-quarters fill the baking pan with the almond dough.
Cover the surface with some whole almonds. Bake in an oven at temperature 345°F (175°C)
for about 35 minutes. Let the frangipane tart with black cherries cool completely
before turning it out, then dust the surface with powdered sugar.

Preparation: 35' - Cooking: 35'
Difficulty: medium

GIANDUJA TART
WITH EXTRA-VIRGIN
OLIVE OIL

INGREDIENTS FOR 4-6 PEOPLE

**For the shortcrust pastry
with extra-virgin olive oil**
(see page 11)
1 cup (125 g) of white flour
4 tbsp + 1 tsp (65 g) of brown
sugar
2 tbsp + 1 tsp (35 ml) of
extra-virgin olive oil

2 tbsp (30 ml) of water
1 tsp (3 g) of baking powder
grated lemon zest
vanilla

For the filling
9 oz (250 g) of dark chocolate

3 tbsp + 1 tsp (50 g) of
hazelnut paste
2 tbsp (30 ml) of light extra-
virgin olive oil

For the finishing
cocoa
hazelnuts

PREPARATION

For the shortcrust pastry, dissolve the sugar in cold water and knead all the ingredients together.
Leave in the refrigerator for at least an hour. Roll out the shortcrust pastry on a floured pastry board with
a rolling pin to a thickness of 0.12 in (3 mm). Line a baking pan of 8 in (20 cm) diameter which has previously
been oiled and floured. Bake it and cook before filling, placing inside, covered with greaseproof paper,
dried legumes or rice (you can re-use them many times), at 350°F (180°C) for 18-20 minutes.
Turn out and leave to cool, then remove the tart from the pan. For the filling, chop up the chocolate,
melt it bain-marie or in the microwave. Add the hazelnut paste and then the oil to the chocolate,
being careful to choose a light and delicate type of oil. Mix well, until everything is lukewarm and begins
to thicken, then pour into the tart, putting a little aside, and allow it to set. Whip the remaining
cream with a whisk until it is soft and foamy and garnish the tart using a pastry bag.
Decorate with hazelnuts and dust with cocoa. Leave to set, at least
for an hour before serving, in cool air, preferably not in the refrigerator.

Preparation: 1 h - Cooking: 18'-20'
Cooling: 1 h - Difficulty: medium

MARBLE
TART

INGREDIENTS FOR 4-6 PEOPLE

9 oz (250 g) of cocoa shortcrust
pastry (see page 11)

4.4 oz (125 g) of white chocolate
3.5 oz (100 g) of dark chocolate

For the filling
3/4 cup + 4 tsp (200 ml) of cream
2 tsp (10 g) of glucose syrup

For the finishing
0.7 oz (20 g) of sliced toasted
almonds

PREPARATION

Roll out the shortcrust pastry with cocoa on a pastry board with a rolling pin to a thickness of 0.12 in (3 mm).
Line a cake pan of diameter 8 in (20 cm), which has been buttered and floured.
Place inside it dried legumes, covered with oven paper, and rice and bake it and cook before filling, placing
inside (you can re-use them many times) in an oven a a temperature of 350°F (180°C) for about 20 minutes.
Turn it out and let it cool, then remove the tart from the pan.
For the filling, chop up the white and dark chocolates and put them in two bowls.
Boil the cream with the glucose syrup in a small saucepan and pour half into each chocolate.
Mix well until you obtain two smooth and velvet creams. Pour the two *ganache* into the tart
and mix lightly with a knife to obtain the marble effect.
To finish, sprinkle the edge of the marble tart with two chocolates with the sliced almonds,
and put the tart in the refrigerator to hardenfor at least one hour.

Preparation: 1 h - Cooking: 18'-20'
Cooling: 1 h - Difficulty: medium

MINI RICE TARTS

INGREDIENTS FOR 6 PEOPLE

11 oz (300 g) of shortcrust pastry
(see page 11)

For the filling
3 cups (750 ml) of milk
3/4 cup (150 g) of rice
1/2 cup + 3 tbsp (150 g) of sugar
2 eggs

2 egg yolks
1/2 grated lemon zest
1/2 small glass liqueur with aniseed
(or other of your choice)

For the finishing
10 tsp (50 g) of gelatin
for desserts

PREPARATION

Cook the rice with the milk and the sugar in a saucepan on a medium flame for about 40 minutes.
Leave it to cool, then add the eggs, the yolks, the liqueur and the grated lemon zest.
Pour everything into 6 small baking tins 4 in (10 cm) in diameter, previously covered in shortcrust pastry
extended with the rolling pin to a thickness of 0.12 in (3 mm).
Bake in an oven at temperature 350°F (180°C) for 35 minutes, until the crust is yellow and crisp.
Leave the rice tarts to cool completely before turning them out.
Finally, apply gelatin for desserts.

Preparation: 1 h - Cooking: 35'
Difficulty: easy

LITTLE FRANGIPANE TARTS

INGREDIENTS FOR 4 PEOPLE

7 oz (200 g) of almond shortcrust
pastry (see page 12)

1 egg
1.5 tbsp (20 g) of type "00" flour
4 tbsp (60 g) of apricot jam

For the filling
3 tbsp + 1 tsp (50 g) of butter
5 tbsp (60 g) of powdered sugar
1.7 oz (50 g) of almonds

For the finishing
almonds grain
powdered sugar

PREPARATION

Grind the almonds finely in a mixer, stopping and starting.
Mix the butter and the powdered sugar in the planetary mixer with flat beater, then add the almond powder.
Add the egg and then the sieved flour.
Line two cake tins of about 4 in (10 cm) diameter with the shortcrust pastry, rolled out
to a thickness of 0.12 in (2-3 mm), then spread apricot jam on the bottom and fill to three quarters
with the almond dough. Cover the surface with almonds grain and dust with powdered sugar.
Bake in an oven at temperature 345°F (175°C) for about 20 minutes.
Let the frangipane tarts cool completely before turning them out.

Preparation: 35' - Cooking: 20'
Difficulty: medium

NEAPOLITAN PASTIERA

INGREDIENTS FOR 4 PEOPLE

For the pastry (see page 11)
1 + 1/2 cup (200 g) of type "00" flour
7 tbsp (100 g) of butter
7 tbsp (100 g) of sugar
1/2 tsp (2 g) of baking powder
1 egg
zest of 1 lemon
a pinch of salt

For the filling
1 cup + 2 tbsp (250 g) of ricotta
6 tbsp (75 g) of powdered sugar
1 cup (225 g) of custard
1 egg yolk
10 tbsp (150 g) of cooked wheat grain for pastiera
1.7 oz (50 g) of candied citron
orange flower water

PREPARATION

In a pie dish, mix the butter softened at room temperature with the sugar, add the eggs and the grated lemon zest and a pinch of salt. Then add the sieved flour together with the baking powder and complete the pastry. Leave the pastry in the refrigerator for at least an hour.
Then roll it out to a thickness of 0.16 in (3-4 mm) with a rolling pin on a floured pastry board.
Line the bottom of a baking tin with the pastry (you can keep a little pastry on one side, if you want to decorate the surface of the pastiera, once the filling is poured).
Sieve the ricotta with the powdered sugar. In pie dish, combine the ricotta with the custard, the yolks, the cooked grain, the citron cut into small cubes and the scent of the orange flowers.
Pour the filling into the inside of the baking pan. Cover as you wish with strips of pastry and bake at a temperature of 350°F (180°C) for about 40 minutes.
Leave the Neapolitan pastiera to cool completely, before turning it out.

Preparation: 50' - Rest: 1 h
Cooking: 40' - Difficulty: medium

PIES AND SHORTCRUST CAKES

BANANA CREAM PIE

INGREDIENTS FOR 4 PEOPLE

9 oz (250 g) of cocoa shortcrust pastry
(see page 11)

For the filling
2 egg yolks
5 tbsp (75 g) of sugar
1.5 tsp (20 g) of type "00" flour
1 cup (250 ml) of milk
1 vanilla bean

1 leaf of fish glue
12 oz (350 g) of bananas
1/2 lemon

For the Italian meringue
2 whites of egg
8 tbsp (125 g) of brown sugar
2 tbsp (30 ml) of water

PREPARATION

Heat the milk in a pan with the vanilla cut with a knife. Beat yolks and sugar in a container, then add the sieved and flour and mix. Pour a little milk on the eggs to melt into them, then add the rest and melt well. Put them in the pan and bring to the boil. Add the fish glue, softened and then squeezed, and mix. Allow to cool. Line a baking tin 8 in (20 cm) in diameter with the shortcrust pastry rolled out to a thickness of 0.12 in (3 mm). Bake, placing inside, covered with greaseproof paper, dried legumes or rice, at 350°F (180°C) for 20 minutes. Let the bottom of the tart cool before turning it out. Peel the bananas and whisk them with the lemon juice. Add them to the cream, almost cold. Pour everything into the pre-cooked tart and place in the refrigerator for an hour. For the Italian meringue, in a small saucepan, preferably copper, cook 7 tbsp (110 g) of sugar with the water. In the meantime, whip the white with the remaining 1 tbsp (15 g) of sugar. When the sugar has reached 250°F (121°C), drizzle it into the whipped whites of egg and whip until it cools. Decorate with the meringue, using a pastry bag, and flame with the appropriate device.

Preparation: 50' - Cooking: 20'
Rest: 1 h - Difficulty: medium

PUMPKIN AND HAZELNUT PIE

INGREDIENTS FOR 4 PEOPLE

9 oz (250 g) of hazelnut shortcrust
pastry (see page 12)

For the filling
18 oz (500 g) of pumpkin
3/4 cup + 4 tsp (200 ml) of cream
2 tbsp + 1 tsp (30 g) of type "00" flour

2 egg yolks
5 tbsp + 1 tsp (80 g) of sugar
3.5 oz (100 g) of toasted hazelnuts
zest of 1/2 lemon
1/2 vanilla bean
powdered sugar

PREPARATION

Wash the pumpkin, cut off skin then cut into pieces and cook it in the oven at a temperature of 350°F (180°C) for about half an hour or until it is soft. If it should become too brown, cover it with a sheet of tinfoil. Let it cool, get rid of seeds and threads, then put it through a vegetable mill or a food mixer. Beat the yolks and the sugar in a bowl with a whisk, then combine the sieved flour and mix well. In a small saucepan, boil the cream with the vanilla bean cut with a small knife, then pour it onto the beaten yolks, mixing well with the whisk; put everything in the small saucepan and cook like a normal custard. Allow to cool well, after having eliminated the vanilla, and mix with the pumpkin cream. Scent everything with the grated lemon zest. Line a baking tin of 7-8 in (18-20 cm) diameter with the hazelnut shortcrust pastry, rolled out to 0.12 in (3 mm) thickness. Fill with the mixture and level it well. Sprinkle the surface with the chopped toasted hazelnuts and dust abundantly with powdered sugar. Bake at 350°F (180°C) for about half an hour. Allow to cool completely before turning out.

Preparation: 45' - Cooking: 30'
Difficulty: medium

LIME MERINGUE PIE

INGREDIENTS FOR 4-6 PEOPLE

9 oz (250 g) of shortcrust pastry
(see page 11)

3 tbsp + 1 tsp (50 g) of cornstarch
grated zest of 3 limes
1 leaf of fish glue

For the filling
4 tbsp + 1 tsp (65 ml) of lime juice
3/4 cup (180 g) of butter
1/2 cup + 3 tbsp (150 g) of sugar
7.5 tbsp (100 g) of powdered sugar
7 egg yolks

For the Italian meringue
2 whites of egg
1/2 cup + 1 tbsp (125 g)
of brown sugar
2 tbsp (30 ml) of water

PREPARATION

Line a baking tin of about 8 in (20 cm) diameter with the shortcrust pastry rolled out to a thickness
of 0.12 in (3 mm). Bake in an oven at temperature 350°F (180°C) for about 20 minutes.
Boil the juice and the grated zest of the limes with the butter and sugar.
Beat the yolks with the powdered sugar, than add the sieved cornstarch. Pour into the mixture and cook
until it boils again, beating well. Add the gelatin, softened in cold water and squeezed, and mix until it is
completely dissolved. Cool the cream rapidly, by pouring it into a large pyrex dish and stirring occasionally.
Fill the already-cooked shortcrust pastry bottom with the lime cream, then let it set in the refrigerator
for 2 hours. Begin to cook 1/2 cup (110 g) of sugar with the water in a small saucepan, preferably copper.
In the meantime, begin to whip the whites of egg with the remaining 1 tbsp (15 g) of sugar.
When the sugar has reached 250°F (121°C), drizzle it into the whipped egg whites
and beat until it is cool. Decorate the tart with meringue and flame it
with the appropriate device.

Preparation: 30' - Cooking: 20'
Rest: 2 h - Difficulty: medium

BLUEBERRY PIE

INGREDIENTS FOR 4-6 PEOPLE

14 oz (400 g) of shortcrust pastry
(see page 11)

2 tbsp (30 g) of rice flour
2 tbsp (30 g) of potato starch
1/2 lemon

For the filling
18 oz (500 g) of blueberries
7 tbsp (100 g) of sugar

For the finishing
powdered sugar

PREPARATION

Wash and dry the blueberries on kitchen paper (if you use frozen blueberries,
let them thaw and drain them of the liquid). In a bowl, mix the sugar with the starch and rice flour.
Mix the blueberries with the sugar and starch, then add the lemon juice.
Line a baking tin of about 8 in (20 cm) diameter with a little more than half the shortcrust pastry
rolled out to a thickness of 0.12 in (3 mm).
Fill with the blueberry filling, cover with the rest of the pastry and seal the edges well.
Pierce the surface with a toothpick or the prongs of a fork to allow vapor formed during cooking to escape.
Bake at temperature 350°F (180°C) for about 45 minutes.
Take out of the oven and allow to cool completely before you turn it out.
Serve the blueberry shortcrust tart with a dusting of powdered sugar.

Preparation: 30' - Cooking: 45'
Difficulty: easy

PIE WITH
AMARETTO FILLING

INGREDIENTS FOR 4-6 PEOPLE

14 oz (400 g) of shortcrust pastry
(see page 11)

For the finishing
powdered sugar

For the filling
3/4 cup (180 g) of plum jam
2 oz (65 g) of *amaretti*

PREPARATION

Line a baking pan of about 8 in (20 cm) diameter with the shortcrust pastry rolled out
to a thickness of 0.12 in (3 mm).
Spread a layer of plum jam on the bottom of the baking pan. Place the *amaretti* side by side on the jam.
Roll out the remaining pastry and cover the surface.
Seal the edges and make some little holes with a toothpick or the prongs of a fork,
to allow the vapor formed during cooking to escape.
Bake at a temperature of 350°F (180°C) for about 20-25 minutes.
Let the shortcrust tart cool completely before turning it out.
Dust the shortcrust tart with *Amaretto* filling with powdered sugar.

Preparation: 25' - Cooking: 20'-25'
Difficulty: easy

LEMON CREAM PIE

INGREDIENTS FOR 4-6 PEOPLE

14 oz (400 g) of shortcrust pastry
(see page 11)

6 tbsp (90 g) of sugar
1 tbsp + 1 tsp (18 g) of potato starch
1 lemon

For the filling
1/2 cup (125 ml) of milk
4 tbsp + 1 tsp (65 ml) of cream
2 egg yolks

For the finishing
powdered sugar

PREPARATION

For the filling, boil the milk and cream. Beat the yolks with the sugar, then add the sieved potato starch.
Pour into the previous mixture and cook until it boils again, beating well.
Allow the cream to cool rapidly, pouring it into a large pyrex dish and mixing from time to time,
then add the lemon juice and grated zest.
Divide the shortcrust pastry into two parts, one slightly larger then the other,
and from it make two disks of 0.12 in (3 mm) thickness with a rolling pin.
Line a baking pan of about 8 in (20 cm) diameter with the larger disk.
Fill the shortcrust pastry bottom with the lemon cream and cover it with a second disk of pastry.
Pierce the surface with a toothpick or a fork to allow the vapor forming during cooking to escape.
Bake at a temperature of 350°F (180°C) for about 25-30 minutes.
Allow the shortcrust pastry tart with lemon cream filling to cool completely, turn it out
and then decorate it with a dusting of powdered sugar.

Preparation: 30' - Cooking: 25'-30'
Difficulty: easy

PIE WITH PINEAPPLE
AND MINT FILLING

INGREDIENTS FOR 4-6 PEOPLE

14 oz (400 g) of shortcrust pastry
(see page 11)

5 tbsp (70 g) of sugar
4 tbsp (50 g) of cornstarch
about 10 mint leaves

For the filling
a fresh pineapple of about
2.2 lb (1 kg)

For the finishing
powdered sugar

PREPARATION

Peel the pineapple, discard the central fibrous part and cut it into fingers.
Mix the sugar and the starch in a bowl. Wash, dry and chop up some fresh mint leaves.
Mix the pineapple and the sugar and starch mixture and the chopped mint.
Divide the shortcrust pastry into two parts, one slightly larger then the other,
and from it make two disks of 0.12 in (3 mm) thickness with a rolling pin.
Line a baking pan of about 8 in (20 cm) diameter with the larger disk.
Fill with the pineapple filling, cover with the rest of the shortcrust pastry and seal
the edges well. Pierce the surface with a toothpick or the prongs of a fork to allow the vapor forming
during cooking to escape. Bake at temperature 350°F (180°C) for about 45 minutes.
Take out of the oven and allow to cool completely before turning out.
Serve the shortcrust tart with pineapple and mint filling with a dusting of powdered sugar.

Preparation: 30' - Cooking: 45'
Difficulty: easy

PIE WITH
STRAWBERRY FILLING

INGREDIENTS FOR 4-6 PEOPLE

14 oz (400 g) of shortcrust pastry
(see page 11)

4.5 tbsp (60 g) of cornstarch
1/2 lemon
0.9 oz (25 g) of pistachios grain

For the filling
21 oz (600 g) of strawberries
7 tbsp (100 g) of sugar

For the finishing
powdered sugar

PREPARATION
Wash and clean the strawberries and dry them. Cut them in 4 and wet them
with the lemon juice. In a bowl, mix the sugar and the starch.
Mix the strawberries with the mixture of sugar and starch and with the pistachios grain.
Divide the shortcrust pastry into two parts, one slightly larger then the other,
and from it make two disks of 0.12 in (3 mm) thickness with a rolling pin.
Line a baking pan of about 8 in (20 cm) diameter with the larger disk.
Fill with the strawberry filling, cover with the rest of the pastry and seal the edges well.
Pierce the surface with a toothpick or a fork, to allow the vapor formed during cooking to escape.
Bake at a temperature of 350°F (180°C) for about 45 minutes.
Take out of the oven and allow to cool completely before turning out.
Serve the shortcrust tart with a dusting of powdered sugar.

Preparation: 30' - Cooking: 45'
Difficulty: easy

APPLE PIE

INGREDIENTS FOR 4-6 PEOPLE

14 oz (400 g) of short pastry
(see page 12)

1/2 lemon
powdered cinnamon
powdered nutmeg

For the filling
2 lbs (750 g) of apples
2 tbsp + 1 tsp (35 g) of sugar
5 tsp (25 g) of brown sugar
3.5 tbsp (50 g) of cornstarch

For the finishing
2 tsp (10 ml) of water
3 tbsp + 1 tsp (50 g) of sugar

PREPARATION

In a bowl, mix the sugars and the starch, a little cinnamon and nutmeg and the grated lemon zest.
Peel the apples and discard the core, cut them in half and make 0.08-0.12 in (2-3 mm) thick slices.
Place them in container and wet them with the lemon juice. Add the mixture of sugars, starch and spices and
mix well. Divide the shortcrust pastry into two parts, one slightly larger then the other, and from it make
two disks of 0.12 in (3 mm) thickness with a rolling pin. Line a baking pan of about 8 in (20 cm) diameter with
the larger disk. Fill with the apples, cover with the rest of the shortcrust pastry and seal the edges well.
Pierce the surface with a toothpick or a fork, to allow the vapor formed during cooking to escape.
Bake at a temperature of 350°F (180°C) for about 45 minutes.
In the meantime, boil the water and sugar to obtain the syrup to gloss the tart.
Take it out of the oven, brush with the syrup and bake again at 435°F (220°C) for about 5 minutes.
Allow the apple pie cool completely before turning it out.

Preparation: 30' - Cooking: 50'
Difficulty: easy

APPLE PIE
WITH ALMOND STRUDEL

INGREDIENTS FOR 4-6 PEOPLE

10 oz (300 g) of shortcrust pastry
(see page 11)

For the filling
25 oz (700 g) of apples
1.7 oz (50 g) of raisins
7 tbsp (100 g) of apricot jam
1 vanilla bean
1 lemon

For the chopped almond
6 tbsp (90 g) of sugar
1 oz (30 g) of almonds
1/2 cup (120 g) of butter
2 tsp (10 g) of white of egg
12 tbsp (160 g) of type "00" flour
1/3 tsp (1.5 g) of baking powder

For the finishing
powdered sugar

PREPARATION

For the chopped almond, grind the sugar and the almonds in a mixer. Knead the soft butter with the resulting powder and the white of egg, and add the sieved flour with the baking powder. Leave it in the refrigerator for at least an hour. Peel the apples and grate them with a large-holed grater. Put them in a container and add the lemon juice and zest, the vanilla cut and scraped with a knife point, the raisins, softened in water and squeezed, and the jam. Mix well. Line a baking tin of about 7 in (18 cm) diameter with the shortcrust pastry rolled out to a thickness of 0.12 in (3 mm), then place the apple filling. Sieve the chopped paste through a large-mesh sieve or a potato masher with large holes and place on the filling. Bake at a temperature of 350°F (180°C) for about 30 minutes. Let the tart cool, turn it out and dust it with powdered sugar.

Preparation: 40' - Cooking: 30'
Rest: 1 h - Difficulty: medium

PEACH
AND ROSEMARY PIE

INGREDIENTS FOR 4-6 PEOPLE

14 oz (400 g) of shortcrust pastry
(see page 11)

For the filling
2.2 lb (1 kg) of peaches (26 oz
[750 g] if in syrup)
7 tbsp (100 g) of sugar (3.5 tbsp
[50 g], if you use peaches in syrup)

4 tbsp (50 g) of cornstarch
1/2 lemon
a sprig of rosemary

For the finishing
powdered sugar

PREPARATION

Wash and peel the peaches, taking out the pits. Cut them into four and wet them with the lemon juice.
Mix the sugar and the starch in a bowl. Mix the peaches with the mixture of sugar and starch
and with the leaves of rosemary, previously washed and dried.
Divide the shortcrust pastry into two parts, one slightly larger then the other, and from it make
two disks of 0.12 in (3 mm) thickness with a rolling pin. Line a baking pan of about 8 in (20 cm) diameter
with the larger disk. Fill with the peach filling, cover with the rest of the pastry and seal the edges well.
Pierce the surface with a toothpick or the prongs of a fork, to allow the vapor forming
during cooking to escape. Bake at temperature 350°F (180°C) for about 45 minutes.
Take out of the oven and allow the tart to cool completely before turning it out.
Serve tart with a dusting of powdered sugar.

Preparation: 30' - Cooking: 45'
Difficulty: easy

ALPHABETICAL INDEX OF RECIPES

ALPHABETICAL INDEX
OF INGREDIENTS

All the photographs are by Academia Barilla except
©123RF: timer image; Angelo D'Amico/123RF: page 8; Yulia Davidovich/123RF: page 2;
digifuture/123RF: page 123; Anna Liebiedieva/123RF: pages 7, 126; monticello/123RF: pages 14, 128;
Maksym Protsenko/123RF: page 5; Vitalina Rybakova/123RF: page 13;
thodonal/123RF: page 125; Valentyn Volkov/123RF: page 10

ACADEMIA BARILLA

AMBASSADOR OF ITALIAN CUISINE
IN THE WORLD

In the heart of Parma, which is recognized as one of the most prestigious capitals of cuisine, in the area occupied by the historic Barilla plant, there stands the Barilla Center, which houses the modern organization of Academia Barilla. Founded in 2004 with the purpose of affirming the role of Italian culinary art, protecting the regional gastronomic patrimony, defending it against imitations and falsifications, giving value to the great tradition of restaurants and food services, Academia Barilla is a meeting place for great professionalisms and competences which is unique in the world of cuisine. The institution organizes cooking courses for those passionate about the culture of food, offering services dedicated to the operators in the sector and proposing products of excellent quality.

Academia Barilla was honored in 2007 with the *Premio Impresa-Cultura* for its activity of promoting Italian gastronomic culture and creativity in the world. Its center was conceived to respond to the needs for training in the field of food and is equipped with the multimedia instruments necessary for hosting large events: around an extraordinary gastronomic auditorium, there is an internal restaurant, a polysensorial laboratory and various classrooms equipped with the most modern technology. The Gastronomic Library holds more than 12.000 volumes on specific subjects and an unusual collection of historic menus and prints on culinary art: the vast cultural patrimony of the library can be consulted on Internet and permits access to hundreds of digitalized historical texts. This avant-garde organization and the presence of a team of internationally famous teachers guarantee a wide range of courses, capable of satisfying the needs both of restaurant professionals and of simple cooking enthusiasts. Academia Barilla also organizes cultural meetings and initiatives to give value to culinary science which are open to the general public, in which participation of experts, chefs and gastronomic critics participate. Since 2012 Academia Barilla has been organizing the Pasta World Championship, in which chefs from all around the world are participating.

www.academiabarilla.it

WHITE STAR PUBLISHERS

WS White Star Publishers® is a registered trademark
property of De Agostini Libri S.p.A.

© 2015 De Agostini Libri S.p.A.
Via G. da Verrazano, 15 - 28100 Novara, Italy
www.whitestar.it - www.deagostini.it

Translation: Jonathan West - Editing: Iceigeo, Milano (Chiara Schiavano, Francesca Gentile)

ISBN 978-88-544-0982-8
1 2 3 4 5 6   19 18 17 16 15

Printed in China

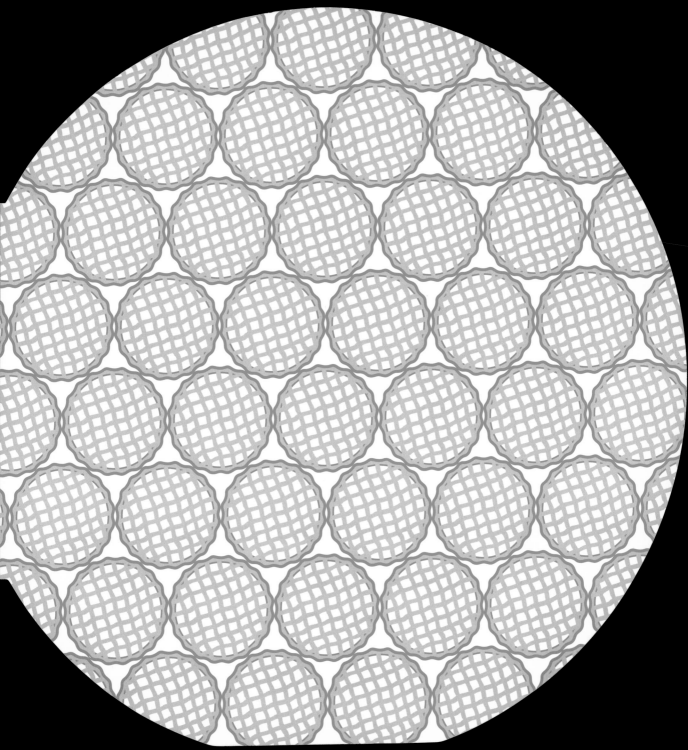

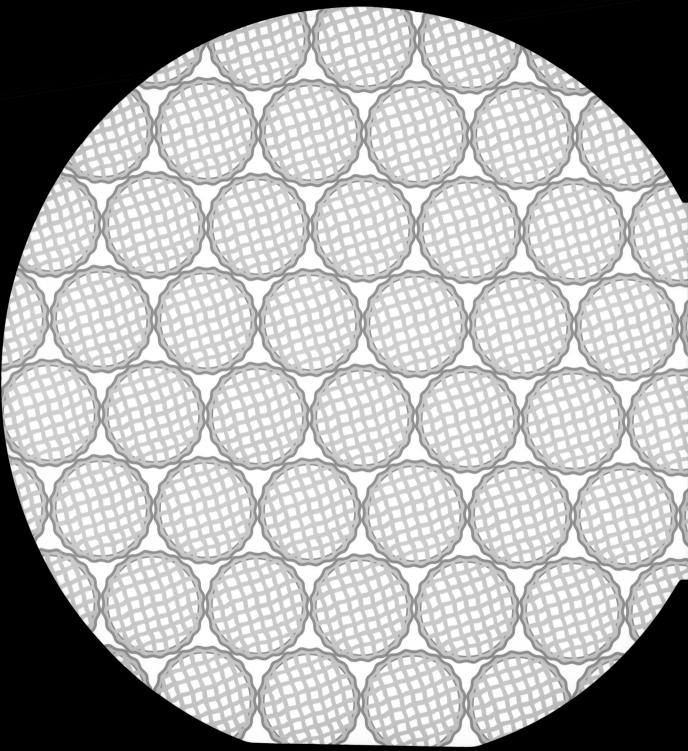